LIVING WITH ACNE

ABDO
Publishing Company

LIVING WITH ACNE

by MK Ehrman
Content Consultant
Joyce Teng, MD, PhD, Director of Pediatric Dermatology
Clinical Associate Professor of Dermatology and Pediatrics,
Stanford University School of Medicine

LIVING WITH HEALTH CHALLENGES

CREDITS

Published by ABDO Publishing Company, PO Box 398166, Minneapolis, MN 55439. Copyright © 2014 by Abdo Consulting Group, Inc. International copyrights reserved in all countries. No part of this book may be reproduced in any form without written permission from the publisher. The Essential Library™ is a trademark and logo of ABDO Publishing Company.

Printed in the United States of America,
North Mankato, Minnesota
092013
012014

 THIS BOOK CONTAINS AT LEAST 10% RECYCLED MATERIALS.

Editor: Melissa York
Series Designer: Becky Daum

Photo credits: Philip Date/Shutterstock Images, cover, 3; Uros Zunic/ Shutterstock Images, 8; iStockphoto/Thinkstock, 13, 32, 36, 38, 52, 62, 66, 69, 82, 90; Beretta/Sims/Rex/Rex USA, 15; Hemera/Thinkstock, 18, 74; SuperStock, 22; SPL/Custom Medical Stock Photo, 25; Blend Images/SuperStock, 28; CORTIER/BSIP/SuperStock, 40; Custom Medical Stock Photo, 42; Shutterstock Images, 48; Warren Goldswain/ Shutterstock Images, 57; Burger/Phanie/SuperStock, 60; PT Images/ Shutterstock Images, 71; Darrin Henry/Shutterstock Images, 77; Fuse/ Thinkstock, 87; Jorg Hackermann/Shutterstock Images, 95

Library of Congress Control Number: 2013945885

Cataloging-in-Publication Data

Ehrman, MK.
 Living with acne / MK Ehrman.
   p. cm. -- (Living with health challenges)
Includes bibliographical references and index.
ISBN 978-1-62403-240-0
1. Acne--Juvenile literature.   2. Skin--Diseases--Juvenile literature. I. Title.
616.5--dc23

2013945885

CONTENTS

EXPERT ADVICE

I am currently the director of pediatric dermatology at Lucile Packard Children's Hospital at Stanford University. A significant percentage of patients in my clinic are teenagers with acne.

Acne is a very common issue for teenagers. It is one of the most common reasons for teenagers to visit dermatology clinics. If you are one of these teens, I have several words of advice for you to keep in mind.

- First, understand how common acne is! It is a hormonal related skin disease—this means that as your hormones are in flux during your teen years, it is only natural that acne develops and flares intermittently.
- Second, there are two simple ways you can maximize your acne's response to treatment: comply with your doctor's prescribed treatment, and be patient! Acne treatment is a process that takes time.
- Many acne patients need a customized treatment regime for maximal response. If your acne's response to treatment is less ideal or when there are unexpected side effects from the treatment, you will need to contact your health provider or providers. There are many options for treatment

available, and your doctor can help you find the right one for you.

Although the condition can be chronic, with proper medical treatment and early intervention it is unlikely you will have permanent scars. And, chances are, you will see improvement before too long. The majority of people do get better after puberty.

—Joyce Teng, MD, PhD, Director of Pediatric Dermatology, Clinical Associate Professor of Dermatology and Pediatrics, Stanford University School of Medicine

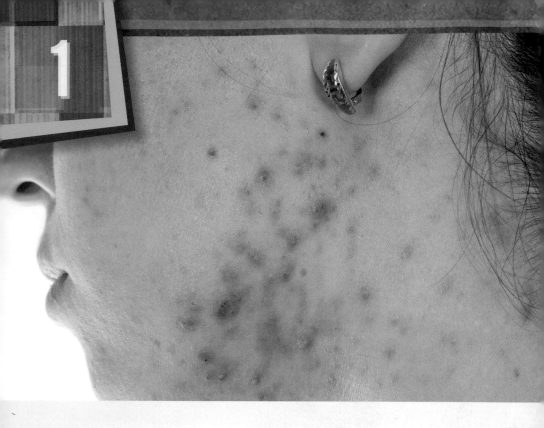

BREAKOUT!

"Ewww!" Jenny exclaimed, looking into her mirror one morning. She blinked her eyes to clear the sleep, but there it was—a big red and white pimple right on her nose. But that was not all. She turned her head and looked sideways and saw more pimples

Sometimes a few pimples multiply into a full acne breakout.

running down her neck. Jenny rotated her body as far as she could and noticed they went down to her shoulders. And rather than the little bumps she was used to seeing, many, including the one on her nose, looked red and irritated.

Things were so busy for Jenny she really hadn't stopped to think about what was happening to her skin. Between schoolwork, the soccer club, and her blog, she wasn't fussing much in front of the mirror. Sure, she noticed a zit showing up here and there, but nothing out of the ordinary. They had shown up before and disappeared just as quickly. Lately, though, they seemed to be sticking around. And there were more of them. And now—she had to be honest with herself—they were everywhere.

"Honey, come downstairs already!" she heard her mother yell. "You're going to be late."

Jenny glumly descended the stairs and presented herself. "Look!" she cried, showing her mother her face, neck, and shoulders. "What am I going to do?"

Her mother had already noticed her once clear-skinned daughter had started breaking out. "You know this kind of thing starts happening at a certain age," she said gently. Jenny was approaching her fourteenth birthday. She was already aware of the changes she and her friends were going through. But it seemed things were getting worse. Come to think of it, she could no longer remember the last time her face had been clear of pimples.

"Is it always going to be this bad?" she asked her mother.

"I don't think it's anything too serious," her mother said, although she too realized Jenny had many pimples, and some did look quite irritated. Jenny's mother decided it couldn't hurt to have a professional take a look. She wanted to help Jenny's skin heal properly and minimize future outbreaks. "Let's set up an appointment with a doctor who specializes in skin problems," her mother said. "Then we can get a better idea of what's going on and what we can do about it. What do you think?"

Jenny thought it was an excellent idea.

WHO GETS ACNE?

Acne can afflict people of any age, from babies to grandparents. Most acne occurs around adolescence, though it is becoming more common to see children seeking treatment as early as age six or seven.[1] Acne often disappears as teens move into adulthood. Acne affects both genders and all ethnicities in roughly the same proportions.[2] Animals almost never get acne. It is usually a human affliction.

THE ACNE YEARS

There is no question about it. Adolescence can present more than a handful of challenges. It is hard enough making sense of your changing body, raging hormones, and added responsibilities. It is the teen years when many people first struggle with trying to understand who they are and how they can relate to others. On top of all that, adolescence is also the time when almost everyone is most prone to acne.

YOUR SKIN IS AN ORGAN

When you think of the body's important organs—the heart, lungs, kidneys, liver—do you forget to include the biggest one, your skin? Skin is an organ that covers our whole body. It protects the body from outside invaders, helps keep our insides at the right temperature, and gives us a sense of touch. With so many important functions, it is important to know how to properly take care of skin and make sure it is as healthy as can be.

As her mom explained to her, Jenny is certainly not alone in having skin problems. Few manage to make it through their teenage years without at least a few eruptions of varying degrees of severity. But when it is your own face and body covered with pimples, knowing others are suffering the same fate does not provide much relief.

WHAT IS ACNE?

In most cases, it hardly takes a medical school education to recognize acne. Doctors do not typically use any special tests when diagnosing acne, also known as acne vulgaris. However, there are other skin conditions similar to acne that might take a trained doctor to distinguish.

Clinically speaking, acne is defined as a skin inflammation caused by overgrowth and increased activity of the oil glands. The pores, or holes, hairs travel through to get outside the body can become clogged by dead skin and other material. There are little glands in the skin that produce oil to lubricate the body hair. Because the oil has no other way to leave the body, it backs up behind the clog, or what doctors call a plug, or comedo. This forms a pimple, or zit. Depending on the nature of the clog and how it develops, a comedo can be a whitehead or a blackhead. These are white-topped or black-topped plugs, which

ROSACEA: "THE OTHER ACNE"

Rosacea is a condition characterized by red, burning skin. Although it is sometimes called acne rosacea because it can produce pimples around the face, rosacea is a separate condition. It has different causes and treatments than acne. It is important to have your skin diagnosed properly for both conditions.

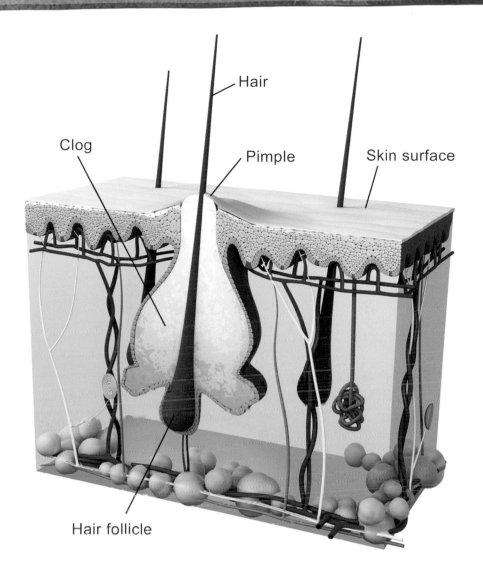

Clog

Hair

Pimple

Skin surface

Hair follicle

Pimples form when hair follicles become clogged.

most people commonly associate with acne. Papules, or small red bumps, can also develop and usually spread over a large area. In the worst cases, these processes result in pus-filled boils or hard lumps called nodules or cysts.

Because many of these oil-producing glands become more active around puberty when people start growing hair in new places, acne is often associated with adolescence. But there are many other factors that can contribute to this condition.

COMPLICATIONS FOR GIRLS

Most of the time, acne is not a symptom of anything else. But in some rare cases, in some girls it can be caused by a serious hormone imbalance. This occurs particularly if acne is accompanied by too much body hair growth, weight gain, or irregular menstrual periods. In such a case, your physician will probably want to conduct further tests before treating you for simple acne.

Even though nobody dies from acne, it should still be taken seriously. Advanced cases can result in the inflammation of large portions of the skin and can lead to permanent scarring. To get through your acne years with as few pimples as possible and with no trace of them once they are gone, at least one trip to the doctor is a good idea. Many teens can simply visit their family physician. However, because of the severity of their condition or their family's health-care plan, some teens visit a specialist, known as a dermatologist.

Visiting a doctor is the simplest way to get the most up-to-date information about what

Acne happens to almost everyone, even celebrities such as Harry Styles of the band One Direction.

exactly is going on with your skin. It is also a good place to learn about the latest and best techniques to manage it. There have been many recent advances in understanding acne, and there are many ways to treat it. It is a good idea to get to know your condition a little better and learn about all the options available.

Once Jenny gets her medical issues squared away, she can also confront the social and self-esteem issues acne can trigger. With both your physical condition and in how you relate to yourself and others, you are not helpless. Your choices do matter. And so does your attitude, so try to stay positive.

Acne is a challenge almost everyone faces. With a little patience and education and a lot of help from friends, family, and other knowledgeable and caring people around you, you can get through it.

FAST FACTS

- Acne affects 40 to 50 million Americans. This makes it the number one skin disorder in the United States.
- If you suffer from acne, you are not alone. Almost 85 percent of people will get it sometime in their lives.
- By the time they finish high school, approximately 40 percent of adolescents will have acne that is bad enough to require a trip to the doctor.[3]

ASK YOURSELF THIS

- *What do you think about Jenny's mother's plan to go to the doctor? How serious do you think we should take an outbreak of acne?*

- *Do you remember your first real outbreak of pimples? When was it? How did you feel? What did you do?*

- *What are some ways you think acne could affect someone's life?*

- *Is there something positive people can learn from the experience of having acne? If so, what?*

2

IS "ZIT" MY FAULT?

"**B**ut-but what did I do wrong?" Darius wondered aloud, after Dr. Sanchez confirmed what he and everyone else already knew—he had a bad case of acne. As the oldest sibling in his family, Darius was accustomed to taking responsibility for whatever happened instead of blaming others. When his head and upper body became peppered with pimples that would not go away, he figured it must be because of some bad habit he had. Otherwise, why was this happening to him?

"Well, Darius, we don't know everything about what causes acne. But we certainly know a lot about what makes it worse as well as what doesn't cause it," Dr. Sanchez said. "And based on everything you've told me, I don't see any reason you should blame yourself."

Dr. Sanchez had spent a lot of time asking Darius questions about his medical history. He particularly asked about when Darius started breaking out, on what parts of his body the pimples appeared, and what products he had tried using to make his pimples go away. The doctor also asked about Darius's diet and if he experienced a lot of stress in school. In fact, the part of the examination when he actually looked at Darius's skin was pretty short compared to all the questions Dr. Sanchez asked him. Darius had offered up many reasons of his own why he thought he had acne, but Dr. Sanchez just shook his head no each time.

"It's good you came to see me, Darius," Dr. Sanchez said. "I know people believe all kinds of things about acne that doctors know are absolutely wrong, and I'm glad I was able to set you straight."

Darius suddenly felt as though a big weight had been lifted off his shoulders. He thanked Dr. Sanchez and got ready to leave.

"Whoa, not so fast," Dr. Sanchez said, laughing. "Aren't you forgetting something?" Darius thought maybe he was about to leave an article of clothing or something else behind. But he quickly realized his mistake.

"Oh, yeah," Darius said, a bit embarrassed. "What are we going to do about it?"

WHY PEOPLE GET PIMPLES

In order to understand your treatment options, you'll find it helpful to have a basic understanding about how, when, and why

BEFORE YOU GO

A little preparation before you visit the doctor will make your examination go much smoother and increase your chances at getting the best care possible.

Write down:

- any illnesses you've had and any conditions you currently have
- all the medications you are taking, whether they are prescription or over-the-counter, as well as any vitamins or supplements you take
- any big changes in your life
- questions to ask your doctor (creating your list of questions in advance can help you make the most of your time with your doctor)

people get acne in the first place. The more knowledge you have, the better you can manage your condition. And just as important, in many cases knowing fact from fiction can also prevent you from unnecessary worry or blaming yourself for your acne, as Darius did.

Scientists understand pretty clearly how pimples form. But the deeper question of why some people get hardly a blemish while others spend years of their lives covered in acne has skin health professionals a bit baffled. Similarly, doctors and researchers do not always understand why a patient might go days and weeks without much of a problem and then suddenly face an eruption of pimples.

However, some of the key players in this condition have been identified. As research uncovers more about how these elements work, doctors are able to design better treatments. They are also able to determine which activities, foods, and products to avoid. Research has also dispelled many longstanding acne myths.

HORMONES

One big culprit in the formation of acne is hormones. In particular, a type of hormone called androgens plays a main role. Androgens, particularly testosterone, the best-known androgen, are sometimes thought of as a male hormone since they play a large role in a boy's

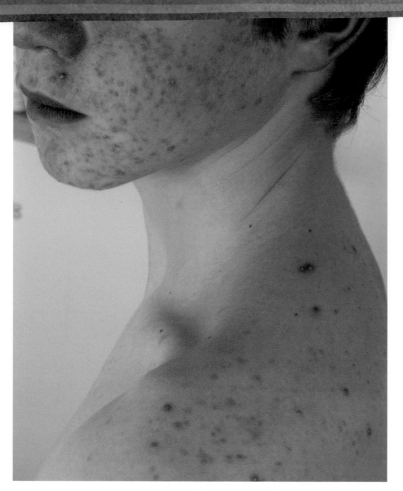

Hormonal changes can lead to acne.

development into a man. However, girls and women have this hormone, too. Having too high an androgen count or a greater sensitivity to normal levels of androgens causes the glands in your skin to grow and produce more oil, in the form of the waxy substance sebum. Sebum is normally the body's friend, keeping hair and skin lubricated and waterproof, among many other functions. However, when it builds up inside a clogged pore, it can lead to acne.

The delicate relationship between healthy skin and androgens means many medicines that affect these hormones can likewise affect acne, particularly hormonal birth control, steroids, and drugs used to treat certain medical and psychological conditions. Additionally, many post-pubescent girls find the ebb and flow of their acne follows a pattern similar to their menstrual cycles. Pregnant women, who also undergo dramatic hormonal changes, are prone to acne as well.

BACTERIA

Another element figures into how blocked sebum can turn into acne: bacteria. *Propionibacterium acnes*, or *p. acnes*, is always living in your skin's pores. It feeds on oils produced in the skin, particularly sebum. Under normal circumstances, that is not a problem. But because the bacteria prefers an environment

ACNE TIME OF THE MONTH

Many girls find their natural menstrual cycles cause many changes in their body, mind, and mood. One of these is menstrual acne. Menstrual acne is an outbreak that occurs seven to ten days prior to a period beginning. When menstruation begins, new pimples stop forming. Menstrual acne is associated with high levels of the hormone progesterone, which occurs about halfway through the menstrual cycle. Approximately 63 percent of acne-prone females are known to get menstrual acne.[1]

BACTERIA: THE GOOD, THE BAD, AND THE ACNE

In a recent study, scientists have discovered *p. acnes* comes in many varieties—some good and some bad. Some types only showed up in people with acne, while others only showed up in people with clear skin. That means not all *p. acnes* bacteria actually cause acne. It also suggests some bacteria even help prevent pimples. By learning more about how these bacteria function, dermatologists hope to create even better treatments for acne outbreaks. These treatments would zero in on the "bad" acne and leave the good ones to help the skin stay healthy.

without air, a clogged pore filled with sebum becomes the perfect environment for the bacteria to multiply out of control. As it does, the bacteria secrete enzymes that break down sebum. This process weakens and irritates the skin cells around the follicle. Immune cells come to the area to clean up, a response known as inflammation. A strong inflammatory response brings with it the biggest dangers of acne, which are permanent scarring and skin color changes.

Even though treating the bacteria will often make the acne condition better, *p. acnes* still cannot be fully blamed for anyone's acne. One reason is that acne can clear up even when these bacteria and their enzymes are present. In addition,

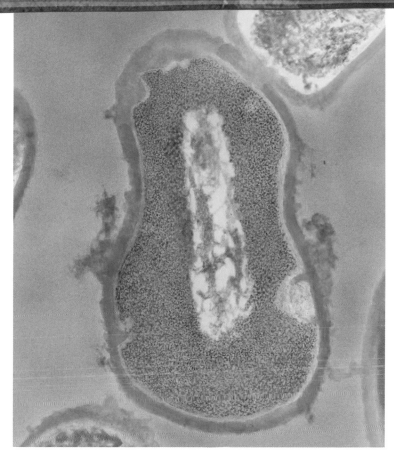

P. acnes *bacteria play a role in acne formation, but they are not fully responsible.*

acne sufferers do not necessarily have more *p. acnes* on their skin than someone with a clear, unblemished complexion.

NATURE AND NURTURE

A major determinant in who gets acne is our parents and grandparents and their parents and grandparents. Acne appears to run in families, and doctors believe there is a genetic component to the condition. However, which

ACNE AND HORMONES

Despite the relationship of hormones to both sexual development and acne, there is absolutely no link between any form of sexual activity or level of sex drive and acne. Some forms of sexual activity, however, are linked to other diseases.

of our genes is the culprit and how and why those genes might make us more vulnerable to acne is still a mystery. Further study is ongoing.

Ultimately, none of the major factors leading to acne are completely under your control. Thus, acne is generally not something you can blame yourself for. Certain behaviors and choices can, however, make a difference in the frequency and severity of your acne. Stress, for instance, appears to be a factor. So it is wise not to stress out about your condition—that could make it worse!

ASK YOURSELF THIS

- Do you think a doctor can tell you a lot about your condition even if he or she does not use a lot of high-tech equipment or medical tests? Why or why not?

- Have you ever blamed yourself for something only to learn it was not your fault? What do you think would be a good way to avoid doing that?

- Does acne seem to run in your family? Have you ever asked your parents or other older relatives about their acne experiences during their teen years? What did they tell you?

- Even if the root causes of acne are mostly out of your control, are there any advantages to knowing what they are? If so, what would those advantages be?

3

BEING A PATIENT
ACNE PATIENT

More than three weeks into her acne treatment, Ava stood at the kitchen sink, a glass of water in one hand and her acne pill in the other. Normally, she would just wash it down and run off to school. But today, she just stood there, hesitating.

It is important to continue your doctor's treatment plan even if you see little progress at first.

"What's the matter, Ava?" her mother asked. "Aren't you going to take your pill?"

When Ava said she wasn't sure, her mother grew alarmed.

"Why? Is something wrong?" she asked. "Are you having any of the side effects the doctor talked about?"

"Oh, no, it's nothing like that," Ava answered. Her mother's question almost made her want to laugh. Because Ava's problem wasn't that she was having side effects. It was that she was having no effects at all! She had followed instructions and took her medication as directed. But still, every morning when she woke up, her pimples were there to greet her when she looked into the mirror. It seemed as though she would have acne forever.

"Why am I even bothering?" she asked. "Is this stuff ever going to work?" Ava shook the bottle to emphasize her point. Ava's doctor had said the treatment required Ava to keep taking the medication until it was gone. From what Ava's mom could hear, there were still plenty of pills rattling around inside.

"Aren't you giving up a little bit early?" her mom gently asked. Ava told her mom a friend at school had her acne clear up after taking pills for two weeks. Ava had already been waiting almost twice as long.

Ava's mom reminded her how the doctor said treatments could take a long time, and she would have to be patient. Different people react differently to medications and not all the acne is the same, he had told them.

"That's right, Ava," her sister Dara said upon entering the kitchen. "You remember how long it took my acne to clear up? They had to try many different kinds of treatments until they found one that worked."

"Well, you're both lucky," her mom added. "Back when I was a teenager, there were hardly any of these medications at all. A lot of us waited years until our acne went away."

Ava thought about what her mother said, then took her pill. She realized she could hang in there for a few more weeks.

BEWARE OF FALSE PROMISES

Acne treatments are estimated to be a $3 billion industry in the United States alone.[1] Not all of the products and treatments sold actually work. Treatment is usually a long slow process. If something sounds too good to be true, it probably is.

NO INSTANT CURES

As hard as it might be for some people to accept, there is currently no surefire "miracle cure" for acne. But this is no reason to despair.

Many advances in treatment have taken place in recent years. A large majority of cases can now be much more successfully managed than they were in years past. The problem is figuring out which treatments will work the best for an individual patient can sometimes be a bit of trial and error. In many cases, you will need the help of a qualified professional.

Generally, what type of treatment a doctor recommends depends on what type of acne you have and how severe it is. Some treatments require you to apply medication directly to your skin. Others come in pill form that you have to swallow, and still others, in very rare cases, involve more serious intervention. Quite a few of these treatments require a doctor's prescription. For many people, however, particularly if the outbreaks are not too severe or too frequent, over-the-counter cleansers and medications will suffice. While these are safe to use on your own, it is still a good idea to get professional advice before starting any kind of acne treatment. Acne scarring is also an issue, and many treatments focus on preventing scars from remaining long after the pimples are gone. Early treatment and prevention are key.

OVER-THE-COUNTER CLEANSERS

For mild cases of acne, the most popular treatments involve gentle cleaning with warm

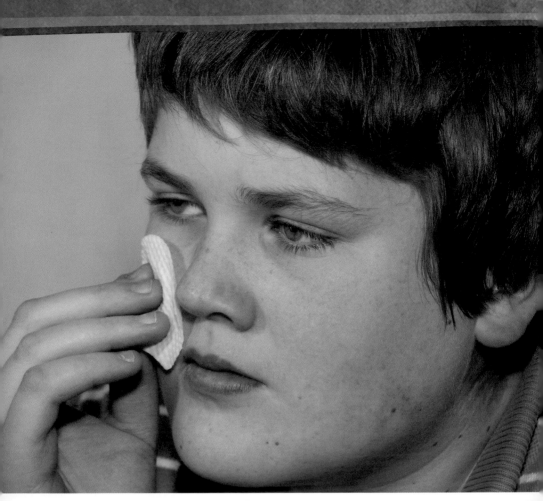

For some people, using an over-the-counter cleanser is enough to clear their skin.

water and a mild cleanser combined with a benzoyl peroxide solution. Benzoyl peroxide has long been a common ingredient in the fight against acne, and it is found in many topical acne medications, both prescription and over-the-counter. It is often effective because the bacteria inside pimples thrive in an oxygen-free environment, and benzoyl peroxide gets inside the pimple and releases oxygen gas, thus killing the bacteria.

Another common ingredient found in over-the-counter acne treatments is salicylic acid, which is the main component of aspirin. Applied to the skin, salicylic acid can reduce the shedding of skin cells from the follicles, thus preventing clogs. Other acids, such as glycolic acid and lactic acid, treat acne by dissolving dead skin cells, which prevents clogs and relieves inflammation. These acids also assist with the healing process and the regrowth of new skin, which may benefit those who are concerned about scarring.

Often, acne patients try products containing the above ingredients first before moving on to stronger acne medications. The advantages of these basic methods are that they are relatively inexpensive and easily obtainable. Their side effects, such as stinging or redness, tend to be mild and short lasting, and allergic reactions are rare.

PRESCRIPTION MEDICATIONS

While some people can successfully treat their acne by themselves with over-the-counter medications, if your acne is inflamed or not responding well to simple treatments, then you might have to look into prescription-strength medicines. In this case, a trip to the doctor is necessary. During the visit, he or she may discuss with you a variety of treatments, either alone or in combination with others, depending on the type and severity of your particular case. One method is to prescribe antibiotics that target the *p. acnes* bacteria. These are usually taken as pills. There are also antibiotics that can be applied directly to the skin if the inflammatory

HELP FROM MOTHER NATURE

Many people today are interested in natural or home remedies over pharmaceutical treatments. These are a few safe and natural substances that may help with acne control:

- Ice: Freezing cold water can help soothe inflamed skin. Holding an ice cube wrapped in plastic on your worst pimples for a few minutes can shrink the inflammation and reduce swelling.
- Tea tree oil: Tea tree oil is nature's infection fighter and healer. Washing with a solution of 5 percent tea tree oil in 95 percent water has been found to be just as effective as 5 percent benzoyl peroxide in combating acne.[2]
- Chasteberry tea: This is effective for girls whose acne is associated with menstruation. There is evidence to suggest this herb helps regulate hormones. Drink it under a doctor's supervision, and do not drink more than one or two cups per day because it affects hormone levels.
- Vinegar or lemon juice: The high acid content of either of these helps maintain clean, healthy pores. Dab a little bit on affected areas next time unsightly blemishes pop up.
- Zinc: Acne is often associated with a deficiency of the mineral zinc. Supplements can help reduce acne breakouts, but only in high doses of 200 to 600 milligrams, so be sure to use this method only under a doctor's care.[3]

papules are superficial and mild. Topical azelaic acid is another common product prescribed for acne to kill bacteria. However, it is primarily prescribed for the skin condition rosacea.

Antibiotics can be very effective, particularly when bacteria are the driving force behind your acne. But they often come with dietary restrictions and other health warnings. It is important you understand all of these instructions when taking these medications.

AZELAIC ACID CREAM

The azelaic acid prescribed to treat acne comes as a cream. It treats acne by killing bacteria and also by reducing the body's production of keratin. Keratin is the protein that makes up the outside of a strand of hair, and it is also found in the top layer of the skin. Keratin can plug pores as sebum does, leading to acne.

Generally, antibiotics are taken for at least two to three months as an initial treatment and then more infrequently and in smaller doses as maintenance.[4] Antibiotics can reduce inflammation, leaving much less chance of scarring. However, continued treatment can lead to antibiotic resistance, as the bacteria that survive these medications will reproduce and pass on their immunity to the new generation.

Not everyone's acne, however, responds to getting rid of the bacteria. Some people

Acne treatments can make you more prone to sun damage, so it is critical you wear sunscreen.

need a treatment that will help unblock their pores, which is something antibiotics cannot do. For that problem, doctors can prescribe a class of medicines called retinoids. These are derived from vitamin A and are believed to help with many skin conditions in addition to acne. Retinoids are usually prescribed in liquid, cream, or gel form. They are applied directly to the skin and reduce dead skin cells clogged in the pore. By opening pores, retinoids can increase the effectiveness of other medications by allowing them to access affected areas at their root. Topical retinoids have relatively mild side effects, such as dryness and irritation to the skin, which typically disappear after the initial use. Retinoids can also increase skin sensitivity to the sun. Therefore, it is very important to wear sunscreen even when the cream is applied in the evening.

> ## DON'T POP!
>
> **To prevent infection and the possibility of scarring, you must resist the urge to pop pimples. In a tiny minority of cases where the inflammation is so severe pressure must be relieved immediately, there is a safe procedure to do so—but only in a doctor's office!**

Most of the time, these prescription medications produce little to no ill effects. But as with any medical treatment, it is important you understand the proper way to take these medications and the risks involved before you begin. And you should always seek medical advice about what to do should any side effects appear. Finally, be sure to prescribe yourself a healthy dose of patience. Acne treatments are often measured in weeks and even months. There are no real shortcuts. But once you get your clear healthy complexion back, you will certainly feel it was worth the wait.

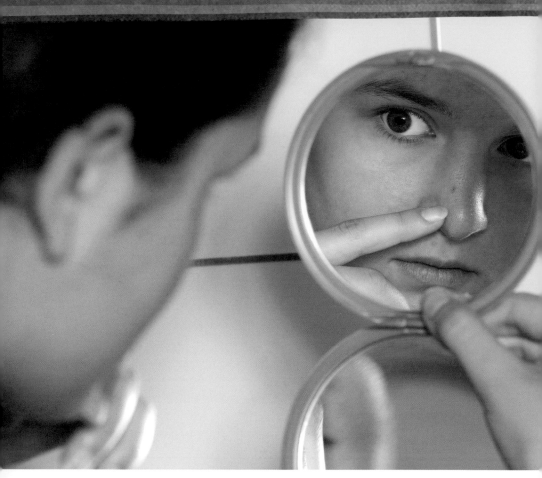

Popping pimples can set back your acne treatment.

ASK YOURSELF THIS

- *Have you ever taken medication for your acne? Has it been effective? How long did you have to wait for results?*

- *Have you ever felt like giving up when something didn't give you results as quickly as you would like? What happened?*

- *What cleansing products do you use? Have you ever tried different products? Have you ever asked a doctor what products he or she recommends for your acne?*

- *Would you take a medication even if there was a risk of unpleasant side effects? What if it worked better than another drug with fewer or no side effects? Why or why not?*

- *Do you think because an acne drug is only available with a prescription it is necessarily better? Or is it riskier? Why or why not?*

SEVERE, PERSISTENT, AND CYSTIC ACNE

Staring up into the bright light, seeing the doctor looking down at him from behind his surgical mask, Hsao could almost believe he was in a movie. In his hand, the doctor held something that looked like a drill. Every few seconds, Hsao saw a flash of light

If your acne is severe or won't go away, your doctor might recommend a surgical procedure.

and felt a little pin poke on his face. Then the doctor's hand would move a fraction of an inch and there would be another little zap. Hsao winced a bit, but really it was more because of the strangeness of the whole experience as opposed to feeling any kind of pain.

When his doctor first mentioned surgery, Hsao was scared. He thought it meant being put to sleep in a hospital operating room and surgeons cutting into him like he had seen on television. But it was nothing like that. He was in a clinic that looked a lot like an office. He was wide awake, and the doctor was talking to him the whole time.

Hsao had been suffering from what his doctor called cystic acne—some of the worst kind there is. His face and back were covered in very large bumps. They were so inflamed, they even turned the skin around them red. And, unlike most acne, this kind even hurt every now and then. Hsao had tried many products, even some prescription medicines his doctor gave him, but his skin got steadily worse.

"I think we need a more serious kind of treatment," Hsao's dad had told the dermatologist when Hsao went in for an examination two weeks previously. It did not take Dr. Tonelli very long to agree. In particular,

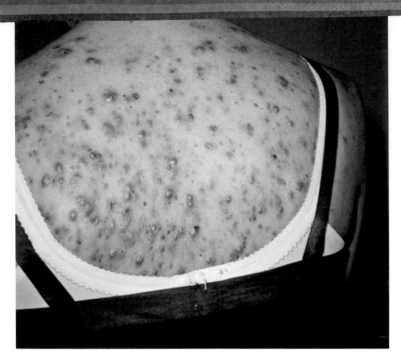

Severe acne can be painful.

the doctor was concerned about scarring. Hsao certainly wanted his acne gone, but he did not like the idea of going to the hospital. "Do I need to have an operation?" he had asked.

Dr. Tonelli laughed. "Not exactly," he said. "It's a simple procedure. We do it right down the hall."

Hsao relaxed and listened to how the dermatologist was going to drain and clean his pimples. For the first time since his acne broke out, he started believing he would get his former face back.

SEVERE ACNE

While basic acne treatments are improving all the time, occasionally they fail. Sometimes more radical intervention is necessary. Often, as in Hsao's case, the acne itself is quite severe. This is usually diagnosed as cystic acne, nodular acne, or nodulocystic acne, all of which are types of inflammatory acne. The ordinary pimples of noninflammatory acne affect a single follicle. However, if pressure and inflammation cause the clog to break out of the individual follicle, the acne is inflammatory. The surrounding cells are damaged, which allows inflammation and infection to penetrate deep into the skin or fuse with nearby comedones. Entire areas of the face, back, and other body parts can turn bumpy and red. These bumps

CYSTIC V. NODULAR: WHAT'S THE DIFFERENCE?

Often you see the terms cystic acne and nodular acne lumped together. In fact, sometimes the condition is referred to as nodulocystic acne. Both cysts and nodules appear as reddish lumps on the skin. The main difference is that nodules tend to be completely solid inside, while cysts are generally a bit larger and are filled with a liquid mix of white blood cells, dead cells, and bacteria. Some acne experts believe cysts are overly inflamed nodules and the conditions are one and the same.

tend to be large, tender, and sometimes extremely painful.

No one is really sure why acne can hit some people so hard it causes cysts or nodules, though as with acne in general, genes and heredity certainly play a role. However, medication has shown a lot of promise in managing even the most severe types of acne. Because of all the damage to skin cells cystic acne causes, scarring is a real danger, so it is important to seek medical advice as soon as possible. Treatment will almost certainly require a physician. Many cystic acne treatments can only take place in a clinical setting—either a doctor's office, or, for more extreme procedures, an actual hospital—and must be performed by a qualified specialist.

ISOTRETINOIN

While topical retinoids are often used to treat mild to moderate acne, they are sometimes ineffective if the acne is too severe. The next step up is the medication isotretinoin, which is taken orally in pill form. Marketed under various brand names, it is often regarded as the most effective acne treatment, succeeding where other therapies fail. Isotretinoin can control oil production, unblock pores, fight *p. acnes*, and reduce inflammation—all the major trouble areas of acne.

However, isotretinoin comes with a lot of warnings. It is a highly controlled substance because it can cause birth defects. It is not usually prescribed unless your doctor sees no better option. People on isotretinoin have reported everything from dry skin and lips to muscle aches and headaches and, on very rare occasions, hair loss. Some people can have mood swings when they are on the treatment. The course of the treatment is typically five to six months, and you must visit the doctor's office monthly to make sure the treatment is continuing safely.[1] In a closely managed treatment setting, isotretinoin can clear up acne with little danger or discomfort. While you are on this treatment, you will be asked to discontinue all other treatments. At the end of the course, you may

iPLEDGE

To control the risks associated with isotretinoin, the US Food and Drug Administration (FDA) set up the iPLEDGE program. The patient, doctor, and pharmacist must all be registered with this program before the medication is dispensed. This program ensures the medication is not used by people at higher risk for side effects (pregnant women, for instance) and that all risks are explained and managed. More information can be found at http://www.fda. gov/Drugs or at http://www. ipledgeprogram.com.

see complete clearing of skin. Unfortunately, approximately 40 percent people will have some relapse, although the relapse is usually not as severe.[2] Occasionally if the acne returns to what it was before, a doctor will recommend a second course of isotretinoin.

EXTRACTION

If acne does not respond to any medication, your doctor may decide direct action is necessary. The most basic form of this is extraction. Extraction is usually done to comedones that are not too inflamed. The goal is to physically remove the clog and the backed-up material from the pimple, relieving the pressure and allowing it to heal as cleanly as possible. In this procedure, the skin around the comedo is stretched tight and the doctor applies pressure using a sterile pen-like device, which causes the backed-up sebum, bacteria, and other gunk to be removed from the pimple.

While this may sound a lot like popping a zit, it is done under precise surgical conditions. If this is done incorrectly, it can lead to a worsening infection and permanent scarring. Even when a doctor performs an extraction, there is some risk of pain and infection. He or she will discuss this with you before deciding on a treatment. Extraction will likely also be used in combination with other acne treatments to keep the pimples from returning.

TREATING WITH LIGHT

For many severe acne sufferers, however, the light at the end of the tunnel is an actual ray of light. Lasers and other forms of light therapy have gained popularity in recent years. Lasers are thin beams of pure, focused light. They had been used in many aspects of skin treatment for years, such as treating birthmarks and scars, before doctors began noticing their positive effect on acne. Lasers come in many varieties. The potassium titanyl phosphate laser (KTP) targets bacteria beneath the skin and kills it, likely by attacking its light-sensitive components. Another type, the pulsed-dye laser, can directly reduce the redness of the skin and perhaps kills some bacteria.

GIVING BACTERIA THE BLUES (AND REDS)

Certain wavelengths of blue light are known to kill acne bacteria. Further research has determined blue light can be combined with red light, which penetrates deeper into the skin, for even better results. While these light treatments are often performed in clinics, the US FDA has approved home blue and red light therapy devices for daily acne fighting between visits. However, these devices are expensive, are not the same as getting treatment in a qualified clinical setting, and provide mixed results.

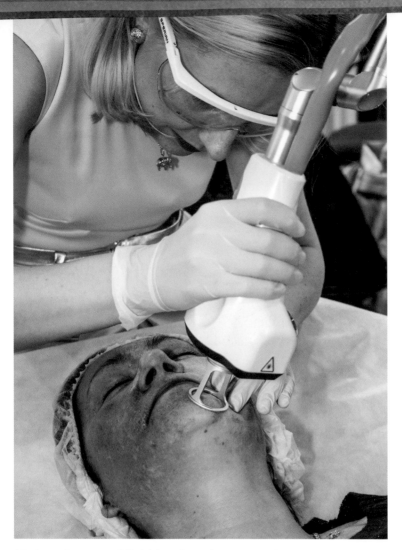

Various laser and light treatments are used to treat acne and other skin conditions.

Other forms of photodynamic, or light-based, therapy use specific color segments of the light spectrum. The light kills bacteria and reduces activity in overactive glands, both of which are major factors in pimple and cyst formation. Sometimes a light-sensitive substance is put on the skin first and activated by the laser for greater therapeutic effect.

OTHER TYPES OF TREATMENTS

Although steroid use is linked to acne formation, doctors may recommend injecting some large pimples or cysts with a diluted form of a class of steroids known as corticosteroids. This is because corticosteroids have anti-inflammatory properties. They can reduce swelling, redness, and pain caused by the cysts and encourage rapid healing. Often, the treated lump simply melts away in a few days.

Sometimes a dermatologist will treat acne by carefully removing the top layers of skin, allowing new, healthier skin to grow back in its place. This process is often done with chemicals, which is called a chemical peel. It is relatively painless, though it often tingles

APPS FOR ACNE

Can mobile phone or tablet applications get rid of pimples? Some companies would like you to think so, and they have actually been marketing apps that claim to cure acne with colored light while you're talking on the phone. While certain clinical devices do treat acne with various forms of light, the light generated by such equipment is many times stronger than what is possible with a smartphone screen. No evidence exists that light from your phone will have any effect on acne. Companies that originally marketed such apps have been forced to drop their claims. Apps you might find helpful are ones that track changes in your skin and pores.

or burns slightly. The skin may look red and feel a little raw or red afterwards, as if you had been sunburned. Generally, you need to avoid sunlight afterward and follow all other healing instructions your doctor gives you.

Just as with moderate acne, no single treatment will perform miracles on severe acne. Even the most high-tech treatments will often be used in combination with other methods to ensure the best possible outcome. So while you may see improvement right away, complete clearance still requires time and patience.

ALL-IN-ONE TREATMENT

Needing more than one mode of treatment is not so bad if they can all be done at once. One recently approved device, called an Isolaz, uses laser light to kill bacteria. At the same time, the Isolaz creates a powerful vacuum that can extract the pimple or cyst, literally sucking it out in a completely sterile environment. After a few hours of redness, the skin returns to normal.

ASK YOURSELF THIS

- *Have you been diagnosed with a type of cystic or nodular acne? How did the diagnosis make you feel? What type of treatment did your doctor recommend?*

- *Have you ever had any high-tech medical procedures? Do high-tech machines give you more confidence or make you more nervous? Why do you think that is?*

- *Why do you think it is important high-tech procedures be done under a doctor's care rather than by yourself, unsupervised?*

- *Have you ever had a medical condition that did not respond to the normal treatment? What happened? What did you do?*

5

SCARRING

By the time Sonia entered her senior year, her acne was pretty much over. The whole time she was in summer camp, she barely had any outbreaks at all. Even by the middle of her junior year, the treatments had started showing results, and her pimples were

Acne can leave raised scars or scars pitting the skin.

fewer, smaller, and less frequent. All of this was something that Sonia should have been happy about. And she was.

The problem was that the acne did not totally disappear. In places where Sonia had the worst outbreaks, on her cheeks and down her neck, her skin was far from smooth. There were little craters, discolorations, and other scars where acne had left its mark. As she looked ahead to graduation, Sonia wondered whether she would ever be able to leave her blemish years behind.

When she had first visited the doctor, he told Sonia there was a danger of scarring. And now, here it was.

The doctor had mentioned it was possible to restore her complexion. Sonia knew friends who got their scars removed. From time to time, she would also see advertisements from doctors and clinics that promised to get rid of acne scars.

"There seem to be a lot of different kinds of treatments," her father said when she brought it up. "We need to look into how we can find the safest, most effective treatment at the best price," added her mother. Sonia agreed to help research. She was excited she might be able to have smooth, regular skin again.

"Once we have a better idea of the options available for you," Sonia's mother continued, "we'll have another discussion and figure out how we're going to pay for it." She explained how these kinds of procedures were considered cosmetic, or not something that was critical to health and well-being. Sonia's dad agreed, explaining these procedures were not covered by the family's insurance policy.

Sonia said she understood. She felt she was getting a better idea of what being grown up was all about.

THREE OUNCES OF PREVENTION

The best way to deal with acne scars is to not get them at all. Here are some prevention tips:

- Early, thorough treatment: Catching acne early and treating it effectively and thoroughly is your best protection against post-acne scarring. This is why it is important to not wait for treatment when acne flares up.
- Keep your hands off: Touching, picking at, and popping zits damages cells, increases inflammation, and allows infections to spread, all of which can increase your chance of scarring. Even too much cleaning and scrubbing can inflame acne. Carefully follow the skin care regimen provided by your doctor or health care specialist, and the rest of the time, leave those pimples alone!
- Know your skin: Some people are genetically more prone to scarring than others. If you have a history of scarring, be extra vigilant with your acne.

SCARS THAT DON'T GO AWAY

You have already heard a lot about the dangers of scarring. But what is scarring? How does it happen? Most important, what can you do about it? As with acne itself, scarring and its treatment is not a one-size-fits-all affair. Acne scars come in many different varieties. Various types of scars have different causes and may respond better or worse to different types of treatments. And similar to acne, multiple treatments are usually required. The process can take weeks, months, or even longer. Unlike acne, however, which in a majority of cases is temporary, many scars can be with you for life if left untreated, even if they do fade a bit over the years.

SCAR CULPRIT: NEUTROPHIL

Scarring is less a result of the acne itself than the body's response to fight off the acne infection. One acne fighter is a friendly white blood cell called a neutrophil. It shows up at the acne infection site and more or less explodes, releasing enzymes and other material that kill off bacteria. However, this reaction can also damage surrounding skin cells. If it recurs often enough at the same location, scarring will result.

DEPRESSIONS

The most common acne scars are depressions. These are the pits, craters, and gaps you often see on people who have suffered from severe and prolonged acne. As a result of recurrent acne, and the resultant inflammation and skin cell damage, the body gives up trying to repair these areas. This leaves an empty space where skin used to be.

Depressions can be classified into three main types. Rolling scars tend to be shallow with an undefined shape, and they leave the skin with a wavy texture. Because the damaged skin is close to the surface, it is relatively easy to treat. Boxcar scars are deeper, with a more defined shape and sharp edges that look almost like corners. The most difficult depression scars to eradicate are the dreaded ice pick scars, so named because the damage is ice pick shaped, with a narrow opening but penetrating deep below the skin's surface.

RAISED SCARS

As with serious injuries or major surgery, in the aftermath of prolonged skin damage from severe acne, the body might not be able to meticulously recreate the network of live skin cells. In these cases, the body simply fills the area with collagen. This is the lifeless, rubbery, red or pink material that most people associate with scar tissue. This results not in depressions but in raised bumps that extend above the surface of the skin, known as raised scars.

Acne often leaves pits or depressions in the skin.

In hypertrophic scarring, the collagen basically replaces the injured skin. Although it is raised up and feels thick and firm, the collagen does not extend much beyond the initial border of damage. Worse are keloid scars. These can be thick, ropey, and often painful. These occur when skin has lost its repair blueprint, so it keeps producing collagen, but of a different

ENTER THE MATRIX

Collagen, the main ingredient of scar tissue, is typically present in the skin as what is called a building matrix. This means it creates a kind of framework for skin cells to form around, resulting in healthy, normal-looking skin. When this matrix is damaged, the body no longer has a blueprint for reconstructing the skin. Instead, it simply pours collagen into the damaged area, which is how a raised scar is born.

kind than with hypertrophic scars. The scar tissue in keloid scars can run well outside the area of the original inflammation.

DISCOLORATION

Sometimes acne can leave behind discolored skin. If the capillaries near the skin surface become damaged or no longer function properly, erythema, which looks like red spots, occurs. Depending on certain conditions and your own natural skin color, the affected area can suffer from hyperpigmentation or hypopigmentation.

Hyperpigmentation is too much coloration. It can occur because too many melanin-producing cells gather at the inflammation site, causing pink or brown spots or blotches. Melanin is the ingredient that gives our skin color. The opposite effect, hypopigmentation, occurs when these melanin-producing cells are missing or damaged in that area. This can leave light or white spots, which are particularly visible on darker-skinned people.

Technically, skin discoloration is not really scarring. It has more potential to fade and even disappear on its own than true scars. But, healing can still take months or years. If discoloration persists, some kind of treatment might be desirable.

WHAT CAN BE DONE?

Many of the techniques used to treat severe acne are also effective at removing scars. And as with acne, more than one type of treatment might be necessary to return the skin to normal, depending on the type and variety of scarring present. Chemical peels are particularly effective for raised scars. Another technique is dermabrasion, in which a rough brush is used to remove the outer layer of skin, allowing new healthy skin to grow. Doctors can also use laser resurfacing, which is basically the same process using lasers instead of a brush

SCARRING BY THE NUMBERS

An estimated 10 million people in the United States suffer from some form of acne scarring every year, although it is often mild. That means 95 percent of acne patients will experience scarring.[1] Fortunately, newer forms of acne treatment are reducing the scarring risk substantially.

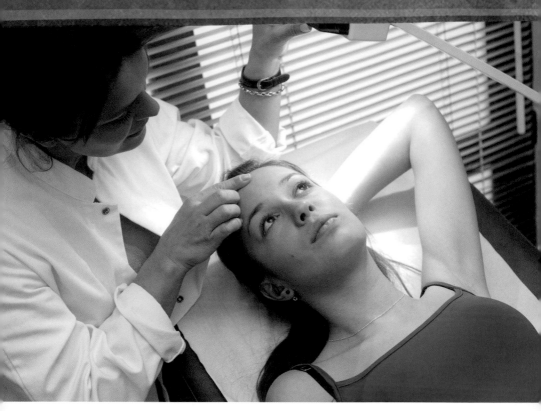

There are many possible treatment options if you notice acne scars that aren't fading.

or chemicals. These treatments can precisely target the scar tissue, allowing the healthy skin cells to fuse together, thus diminishing or eliminating the scar altogether.

In some cases of hypertrophic scars, as with acne itself, the damage can be repaired with corticosteroid shots. The corticosteroid is injected into the scar tissue, causing it to flatten and ultimately dissolve. Sometimes collagen injections are used to fill particularly deep ice pick scars. There are even cases where actual surgery is needed to repair the skin. All methods have limitations and risks. Often the scar simply returns. It is important to get as much expert advice as you can before deciding on a treatment. This is especially true because these treatments are expensive, ranging from hundreds to thousands of dollars. In addition, treatments are generally considered cosmetic, so they are not typically covered by health insurance.

ASK YOURSELF THIS:

- *If you needed acne scars removed, how do you think it should be paid for and why?*

- *What do you think are the most important things to consider when deciding which method to use to remove acne scars?*

- *If you had scars removed, do you think it would improve your life? In what ways?*

- *Do you have any other kinds of non-acne scars? Where are they? How did you get them? How do you feel about having them?*

6

LIVING IN YOUR SKIN—DIET AND LIFESTYLE

After a long run around the lake, Jeremy rested on a bench. Once he caught his breath, he took a long drink of water. He used to be lazy about getting exercise, but that was before his doctor told him how it could help keep his acne under control. That was

Exercise is one healthy habit that can help control your acne.

motivation enough to get him out jogging almost every day. And because his skin needed lots of water to keep clear and healthy, he started drinking as much of it as he could.

Jeremy soon discovered he looked forward to jogging. He also started losing his taste for sugary soft drinks. In fact, a lot about his life had changed. Jeremy understood that to manage his acne properly, he would have to do more than just take medicines. There were little things he could do every day to keep the outbreaks shorter and less severe. He had to be careful about how he shaved and how much sun exposure he got. Jeremy also started eating healthier foods. Above all, he had to avoid touching any blemish-covered areas.

"Man, I don't know if I could do all that," his friend Cyrus told Jeremy. But after a while, it didn't really seem like a big deal. It had just become second nature for Jeremy.

After a few months had passed, the improvement in Jeremy's acne was plain to see. But when Cyrus asked him if now he would ease up on the health food and jogging, Jeremy laughed. He had been exercising and eating well for so long, he had almost forgotten why he started doing it in the first place. He could now be a little less vigilant about things such as what kind of soap he used or other products he put on his skin. But Jeremy had discovered he had more energy, a clearer mind, and was in better spirits than any time he could ever recall. He wasn't sure he wanted to change anything.

Acne management does not stop at medical treatment. It requires that you make some fundamental changes in your lifestyle. The good thing about these adjustments, however, is that many of them not only help keep pimples at bay, but they generally make you a happier and healthier person. And that is good for everyone.

STIMULATING BREAKOUTS

Coffee, nicotine, and other general stimulants also stimulate the sebaceous glands and can lead to more acne. Try replacing them with water, natural juices, and herbal teas.

WATCHING WHAT YOU EAT

It might be frustrating to learn the role of diet in acne is not fully understood. In fact, for a long time, the official opinion was that there was little or no connection between diet and acne. Recently, however, a few foods and eating habits have been found to impact acne breakouts.

While skin specialists cannot point to any specific food or food component as either a cure or a cause for acne, there are a few recommended diet tips that can help with your overall treatment plan. Water flushes out waste and toxins from the body, including the skin, and thereby supports your immune system. This improves not just your skin but your overall health. The health benefits are magnified when you consider that by drinking water, you will likely consume fewer beverages that are less healthful.

Certain vitamins have also been shown to be beneficial in controlling acne. Vitamins are consumed through foods, or when necessary, they can be taken in supplements. Many types of acne medicines use a derivative of vitamin A, but upping your intake of this vitamin naturally through carrots, broccoli, spinach, and many kinds of fish is also beneficial. Acne is often associated with low levels of zinc, a mineral that seems to discourage growth of the *p. acnes* bacteria, so adding zinc to your diet can help, too. Find zinc in seafood, spinach, beef, lamb, and many other foods. Antioxidants, including vitamins C and E, are considered beneficial to the skin, as is the mineral selenium. A diet high in vitamin E, which is found in green vegetables such as broccoli and spinach and various kinds of nuts and seeds, has been shown to improve acne. So has selenium, which is found in brown rice, wheat germ, garlic, eggs, and various kinds of fish. Omega-3 fatty acids, found in certain

Many types of nuts and seeds have compounds that help lessen acne.

fish oils and seeds, are also good inflammation fighters.

Conversely, dairy products have long been considered an acne trigger. While studies have not conclusively shown dairy products have an effect on breakouts, some researchers suspect the growth hormone given to many dairy cows could have a negative effect.

The role of sugars and starches has recently come into focus with acne researchers. This is because the hormone insulin, which the body produces to help metabolize sugars and starches, has been shown to play a role in cellular inflammation, and thus, acne. Researchers are now suggesting a diet with a low glycemic index works well in controlling acne. Thus people who eat a diet with more whole grains, beans, and vegetables and less white pasta, rice, bread, and sugar suffer less from acne.

However, people have individual sensitivities to certain foods or other substances. It is a good idea to keep track of how your body reacts to different foods and skin care products. You might also want to get the advice of a doctor, nutritionist, or other specialist to create a diet that will work best for you.

TOPICAL PRODUCTS

Because acne affects the skin, it is not hard to understand why you have to be extra careful

INSULIN AND THE GLYCEMIC INDEX

Insulin is the hormone that allows sugar in the blood to pass through cell membranes and provide energy to the body. Diabetes is a disease where the ability of the pancreas to produce insulin is either impaired or destroyed. Without insulin, sugars can build up in the blood to dangerously high levels. The glycemic index (GI) is a system that ranks carbohydrates based on their effect on blood sugar level. By consulting the GI, diabetics are able to keep track of how much a given food can raise their blood sugar and how much insulin they would need to give themselves to counteract it. Lower numbers indicate a slow raising of sugar levels, while higher numbers indicate a faster raise. In nondiabetics, the same index would indicate how much insulin the body naturally produces in reaction to those foods. Because high insulin levels are associated with acne, a low GI diet will result in lower insulin levels and may cause less acne.

about what products you put on your skin. For instance, while concealers can be a lifesaver when it comes to hiding eruptions, it is important to choose products specifically formulated to not clog pores. There are many of them on the market today. These products are typically labeled non-comedogenic. Any kind of greasy product should be avoided since it potentially clogs pores. Also watch for any kind of oil in the ingredients of the products you use, including pomades and other products for your hair.

Astringents such as alcohol are also bad because dry skin is more easily inflamed. While too much washing can irritate the skin, twice daily mild cleansing can be beneficial. Soaps and cleansers should be gentle. Avoid anything with scrubbing particles.

If you shave an area covered by acne, use great care. You can also try different types of electric and regular

DON'T FORGET THE SUNSCREEN

Many acne sufferers like to get suntanned because they feel it hides pimples and discoloration. Some people also mistakenly believe sunlight can dry out pimples. But those benefits are short-lived. In the long run, too much exposure to the sun can cause your acne to return, sometimes worse than ever, due to damage caused by ultraviolet rays. While you should avoid greasy tanning oils, do not forget to put on sunscreen that protects you from both UVA and UVB sunlight.

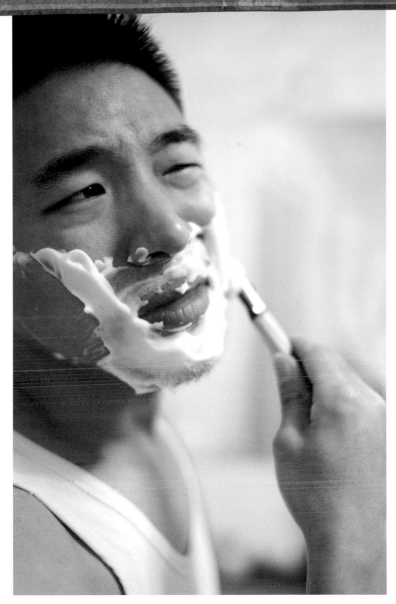

Try different shaving products and methods until you find a process that doesn't irritate your skin too much.

razors and different varieties of shaving creams to see which gets the best results. Likewise, waxing and chemical hair removal can also cause acne flare-ups.

LIFESTYLE

Stress has also been identified as a factor in acne, as both a cause and a result. Any activity that reduces stress can help with your overall acne management. Getting plenty of sleep is one easy way to keep your stress levels down. Exercise is also a great idea. It reduces stress, strengthens your immune system, and brings your hormone levels under control. By improving your blood circulation, exercise makes sure your cells get the oxygen they need and also removes toxins.

HANG UP THE PHONE

Mobile phones are magnets for germs and bacteria. Think about how often you probably touch your phone with dirty fingers and then bring it into contact with your cheek to talk. Because phones also generate heat, they create a perfect environment for bacteria to thrive and multiply. Disinfect your phone regularly with a sanitizer or use a headset.

Because overproduction of sweat, which usually cannot be avoided during exercise, can lead to acne, it is important to wear loose-fitting clothes and shower immediately afterwards. Tight-fitting clothes, headbands, and helmets can worsen acne because of friction. Except for cleansing, avoid touching the affected areas at all. This can spread germs and

Finding ways to relax and reduce stress in your life can help you manage your acne.

inflame already-sensitive skin. It can make acne worse and increase your risk for scarring.

Most of these recommendations—being aware of what is contained in the products you buy, watching your diet, getting exercise, and reducing stress—have many benefits even for people who do not have a problem with acne.

MEDICATION AND LIFESTYLE

Your lifestyle affects your skin and your acne. In addition, it can also interact with your acne treatment. Many antibiotics, for instance, require you to avoid dairy and direct sunlight. Oral retinoids come with their own set of restrictions, including avoiding sunlight and not donating blood, among others. It is very important to follow the instructions given to you by your doctor or health-care specialist.

These restrictions and modifications do not usually need to extend past the time when you are actually involved in the treatment. However, general acne-prevention advice you follow throughout your acne-prone years can also contribute to general good health. It is not a bad idea to continue these good habits throughout your life.

One day, you, like Jeremy, may be grateful for having developed positive healthy habits that will keep you in tip-top shape long after your acne is gone.

ASK YOURSELF THIS

- *How much of your lifestyle would you be willing to change or sacrifice for healthier-looking skin? Are there any foods or other activities that you think you could never give up, even if you had to?*

- *Have you ever had to change the way you ate or the things you did because of something out of your control? What was it? How did you feel?*

- *How important do you think what you eat is to how you look and feel?*

- *Can you think of other advantages to being a careful shopper who reads and understands what is in all the products you buy?*

7

PSYCHOLOGICAL, EMOTIONAL, AND SOCIAL ISSUES

As the top goalie in the league, Rob confidently stood his ground as both fearsome opponents and solid flying pucks raced toward him. But once Rob took off his mask, he felt like a big loser because he had acne.

Acne has a negative effect on some people's self-esteem.

Rob's acne didn't bother him when he was at practice or competing against other teams, but once he had to face himself and others off the ice, his spirits and confidence evaporated. Even the smallest teases and taunts would hurt Rob and send him off hiding. He stopped going to parties and other events, preferring to stay home where no one would see him.

"Hey, aren't you coming out to the victory party?" his teammate Kevin asked Rob after they had won the championship.

"Nah," Rob answered. "I think I'd rather just stay home."

"But everyone is going to be there!" Kevin exclaimed.

Rob decided he could confide in Kevin. "Yeah, I know," he said. "But once the game's over, I feel like everyone is laughing at me and calling me 'pizza-face.' I wish I could wear my goalie mask all the time."

Kevin was surprised to learn Rob felt that way. He tried to tell Rob how his friends and teammates, and even his opponents, respected him. But somehow Rob still could not imagine facing a roomful of people while his face was covered in pimples.

"Well, if you can stand up to a flying hockey puck without flinching, somebody calling you names should be a piece of cake, shouldn't it?" Kevin asked.

Rob thought for a minute and finally said, "Well, when you put it like that . . ."

THE INVISIBLE PAIN OF ACNE

You've heard a lot about the physical aspects of acne. For many people, the real pain of acne is something less visible to medical diagnostics. Some people with acne face name-calling, a lack of acceptance from friends, or a feeling there is something wrong with how they look. Some feel something unfair has happened to them.

ACNE DYSMORPHIA

Mild acne symptoms do not always create mild psychological symptoms. Sometimes people with severe acne can be emotionally well-balanced, while people with only mild acne might find it takes over their lives. In the case of a condition called acne dysmorphia, patients who have only a slight case of acne believe it to be very severe. They can suffer profound depression, anxiety, or negative body image.

Having acne can lead to difficulties with body image, self-esteem, social relationships, and performance at home, school, work, or elsewhere. These issues are often experienced as anger, sadness, anxiety, or the inability to concentrate, depending on the individual. These

Acne can't mar your inner beauty.

feelings have the potential to be even more debilitating than acne's physical effects. This is why it is so important to be aware of these dangers and take effective action against them.

SELF-ESTEEM AND BODY IMAGE

If your skin is covered with unsightly blemishes—particularly on the face and other exposed areas—it might be hard for you to feel your best about how you look. During teen years, when people are struggling with the

MOOD SWINGS

Some acne treatments, oral retinoids in particular, can also cause mood swings. Most of the time, this does not turn out to be a big issue, but should you experience changes in your mental state, mood, or level of anxiety while using an acne treatment, tell your doctor immediately. Your psychological condition may be the result of the medication, not the acne. If you have a preexisting condition, it is important your doctor knows about it before you start a course of treatment. Be sure to follow up with your doctor regularly.

sense of who they are and are extra sensitive about how they are perceived by others, this can be a particularly acute problem. Some people are able to hide the problem, at least in part, with makeup and concealer. But to one extent or another, almost everyone who suffers from acne must confront the way he or she feels inside versus the way he or she might appear from the outside. This can cause problems with forming and maintaining social relationships.

On the plus side, however, having acne is a good opportunity to discover which of your friends like you for who you really are and which judge you based on your superficial appearance. Use the opportunity to move away from toxic relationships.

People form a lot of their attitudes toward themselves and their own bodies during the teen years. Negative thoughts about appearance and identity can be particularly damaging at this time. Therefore, it is important you learn early on not to see yourself and your worth only in terms of your acne.

DEEPER PSYCHOLOGICAL RISKS

In treating the physical complications of acne, the mental effects cannot be ignored. Acne is associated with very serious psychological conditions. Many of those afflicted are prone to depression, extreme social withdrawal, or worse. Anxiety and stress are also associated with acne, both as cause and effect. This leads to a vicious cycle of anxiety and stress making the acne worse, which leads to more anxiety and stress, which leads to worse acne, and so on.

Because acne can cause people to avoid class or work, their academic or

SKIN PICKING

One disturbing symptom stemming from the relationship of acne to poor body image is dermatillomania, or skin picking. According to some experts, people with acne can turn their poor image of their own bodies on themselves, so they pick at their skin. This only makes acne and scarring worse. This obsessive behavior can continue long after the acne years. It primarily affects women. It is believed to have a genetic component and therefore can run in families.

DEPRESSION ALERT

Studies have shown 14 percent of teens with "problem acne" reported feeling depressed, 23 percent said they had thought about committing suicide, and nearly 8 percent said they had tried.[2] If you think acne is doing this to you or to someone you know, get help immediately. Signs to look for include:

- loss of appetite
- low energy, excessive sleepiness
- spontaneous crying
- feelings of low self-worth

job performances may also suffer. Avoiding interaction with other classmates or workers can also have a negative impact. By eroding confidence, acne may also result in fewer job applications, poor job interview performance, and thus fewer job or other opportunities. As clinical psychologist Ted Grossbart explains, "People withdraw and see themselves as uniquely afflicted in a way other people can't understand. . . . Sometimes people will blame their skin for everything that's wrong with their lives."[1]

Similar to many of the challenges of adolescence, the possible emotional and psychological effects of acne can sound scary and daunting. It's important to remember that most people are able to overcome them in the natural course of events. Also, there is evidence that if you follow effective acne treatments, any psychological symptoms are likely to fade along with your pimples.

But if you do feel bad because of your acne, don't try to just cover up the problem. Seek the help of trusted family members, friends, a trusted adviser, or a counseling professional.

ASK YOURSELF THIS

- *How much do you think the way you look matters in how other people think of you? How much emphasis do you place on physical appearance when judging others?*

- *Did you ever think about skipping something you really wanted to do because you were embarrassed about how you looked? What happened?*

- *Do you think acne would bother you as much if it was less visible to others? Why or why not?*

- *What effects of acne have you noticed that have nothing to do with the actual medical problems?*

8

HELP, SUPPORT, AND RESOURCES

"**M**aybe I should just cut off all my hair," Celia said. Her friend Bianca was shocked to hear her say that. Celia was always proud of her long dreadlocks, and Bianca never imagined her friend would even think about getting rid of them. After all, they took years to grow.

"But why, Celia?" Bianca asked. "Don't you like them anymore?"

Celia admitted she still loved having dreadlocks. But recently, her acne was really becoming a problem, and she thought perhaps if she got rid of her hair that would make it clear up.

"But where did you hear that?" Bianca asked. Celia said she had heard people say dreadlocks make acne worse. She was so frustrated with her acne she wondered whether it would be worth a try. Bianca wasn't sure that that was such a good idea.

"Celia, didn't it take you years to grow them?" she asked. Celia agreed it had. "Well, don't you want to make extra sure that's the right thing to do before you do something that will take you months and years to undo?"

The question almost brought Celia to tears. "Everything is so confusing," Celia said. "You hear so many different things, you don't know what to believe. I don't even know where to begin to get good information."

Bianca hugged her friend and told her not to worry. "I think I know where to begin," she said. "Come, let's take a walk."

Celia wanted to know where they were going, but Bianca just said they weren't going far. In fact, they only walked down the hall to the nurse's office. When the girls explained Celia's problem to the nurse, she smiled and said it was a good thing they came to her office.

"I think I know a few places you can look to get you started," the nurse said.

GETTING SUPPORT

Struggling with acne can feel overwhelming sometimes. There are so many different ideas about how to handle it, it can be hard to know whom to listen to and where to look for reliable information. Having acne can make you experience so many moods—including fear, anxiety, depression, and low self-worth—that keeping an upbeat attitude can be a real challenge. At such times, just reaching out for a little sympathy and understanding can make a big difference.

Nobody needs to feel alone. Acne affects millions of teens. And these days there are more ways to get help and support than ever before. Whatever your particular problem or issue is, chances are there is someone who has confronted it too and can help you find a solution.

WHERE TO LEARN

Your first and best source for medical-related acne questions is your personal physician. Not only is he or she an expert on skin care and health in general, but your personal doctor is also directly familiar with your individual situation. Don't be shy about asking questions during visits, and be sure to write down any instructions or advice he or she gives you. If you do not see the improvement expected, your doctor will know which expert you should be referred to. Your school nurse or health adviser can be another good source of reliable information, and he or she may also be able to point you to other good sources to learn more about your condition.

In between such visits, you will have to take a lot of the initiative yourself. You can visit libraries or bookstores where a librarian or clerk can help you find the kind of books you're looking for. Many people turn

CHECK THE DATE

Considering all the recent breakthroughs in acne treatment, it is very important to make sure you're getting the most recent information. If you are looking through printed material, make sure the publication date is less than a few years old. Online can be trickier as not all information posted there is dated. In such cases, you might want to check and see if you can find the same information from a reliable source with a reasonably current posting date.

on their computers and start researching online. For critical medical information or advice on profound psychological or emotional issues, it is important you consult Web sites from established and credentialed organizations, such as the American Academy of Dermatology, the Mayo Clinic, government health departments, major universities, or similar institutions. Be wary of sites that sell skin care products or dermatology services. Some of the advice on these sites might be okay if it is given by a qualified professional, but other information might be posted there just to steer you toward their products or services. It is probably a good idea to have a parent, teacher, or other trusted adult help you navigate your way through all the information available—good and bad—on the Web.

ACNE AND SOCIAL MEDIA

Many people turn to social media platforms to air out problems. This can be okay if you remember the same rules apply as with other forms of online information. Don't accept medical or critical psychological counseling from unqualified or unknown sources. Be aware many social media profiles are thinly disguised advertisements designed to sell products or services. And be sure you know who you're following before you follow them!

Your friends can be a great source of support if you're feeling down.

WHERE TO SHARE

Sometimes you just want to get something off your chest or trade tips and share experiences about different products or treatments. For that, you will find hundreds of online support groups for acne sufferers. Acne.org is one of the largest ones. You can also go online to find support groups that meet in person. And, if there isn't one in your school or neighborhood, you can think about starting your own!

Many acne sufferers keep blogs and post about their struggles with acne. Not only can you read about their experiences but you can usually contact them and ask questions or give them a bit of support yourself. You could even decide to blog about your acne yourself. An even less anonymous way of sharing and receiving information is to post it on social media sites. However, remember that while peer support can be very beneficial, you should be very careful about accepting medical or psychological advice from unqualified people, particularly those who are online and anonymous. Also talk to a parent or trusted adult before sharing personal information or agreeing to meet someone you met online.

ACNE GAMES

Having acne is no fun at all. But there are plenty of online and mobile platform games that allow you to zap zits and watch them disappear. And while it might be frustrating not to be able to pop your actual pimples, there is no harm in doing so to a virtual zit. It might even make you feel a little better.

ASK YOURSELF THIS

- *When you need reliable information, where or to whom do you go first?*

- *Have you ever consulted the Internet for information only to find out the information was incorrect? What happened? What did you do?*

- *With whom do you feel more comfortable talking about your problems: with people you know or anonymously online? Why?*

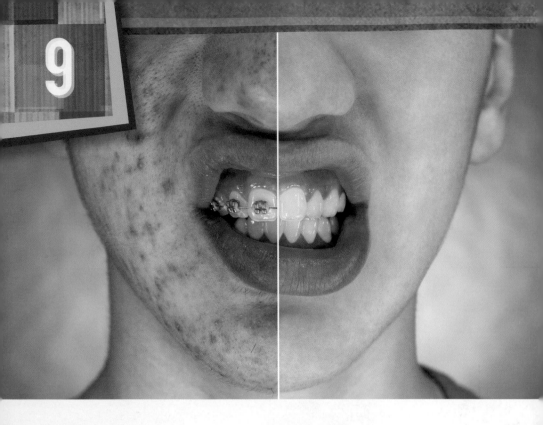

9

ACNE INTO ADULTHOOD

" t looks as though your acne is clearing
up nicely," Dr. Leandro said. "What
seems to be the problem, Dayna?"
Dr. Leandro was surprised to see Dayna
back. It was the summer between high school
and college, which is usually a relaxed and

Your skin will likely clear up as you enter adulthood.

carefree time for teens. And since nothing appeared to be out of the ordinary, the doctor was curious about what might be bothering Dayna.

"What if my acne persists into adulthood?" Dayna asked. "Does that mean I'll have it for life? Will people look at me as if I'm still a kid?"

"Of course, I can't promise that you'll never have another acne outbreak again," Dr. Leandro said. "But the majority of acne cases are people in their teens. If you keep up with your basic healthy diet and skin care regimen, it's unlikely you'll encounter any great problems in the future."

Dayna was a bit reassured, but she still worried about how she would get help once she went away to her university, which was in a different state. Dr. Leandro always seemed to know the latest and best treatments. It wouldn't be easy to return home often for visits.

Dr. Leandro smiled. "First of all, most of what doctors know about healing acne comes from universities," he said. He told her that right now, in research laboratories in universities all over the world, people were working on newer, better, safer, and more surefire ways to treat acne. It was not very likely, particularly in a university setting, that Dayna would be very far from highly qualified medical help.

"But I'll tell you what," Dr. Leandro said. "Why don't you tell me where exactly you're going, and I'll see if I know of a doctor there I can recommend. Would that make you feel better?" Dayna nodded and said that it would.

A VIRUS CURE?

Researchers have recently discovered material from a virus called 11 phage might turn out to be a potent weapon in fighting acne. The virus specifically targets *p. acnes* bacteria. Because the virus also lives on your skin, it evolves right along with the *p. acnes* bacteria, making it more difficult for the bacteria to become resistant to it. The hope is further research will lead to a long-lasting cure.

THE FUTURE OF ACNE TREATMENTS

Research on acne has advanced greatly. There are more treatment options than ever, and the future looks even brighter. It was not very long ago that most teens with acne had little choice but to ride it out and hope their pimples would eventually clear up without bad scarring. During the past decade, however, the landscape has changed considerably. There is still no instant cure that will clear up your skin in a matter of hours or days and prevent pimples from ever returning.

But most people can be effectively treated so they experience shorter periods of breakouts and less scarring. Looking ahead for acne sufferers in general, the odds can only get better.

Time is on your side. By the time people reach their 20s, they are exiting their acne-prone years, and for many, the breakouts subside even without any outside intervention. Of course, your 20s probably seem a long way away if you are barely entering high school. But you don't have to remain idle in the meantime. Current treatments do a good job of controlling acne, often by attacking bacteria, and further research will further distinguish good bacteria from bad. Doctors and researchers also expect that in the future, more treatments will be available that target the inflammation associated with acne, which is the biggest contributor to scarring. Advances in DNA analysis bring scientists closer and closer to breaking the acne code, refining methods of combating acne and even shutting it off at the source. And finally, new technologies requiring special high-tech equipment, such as the various forms of light therapy, may cost more than a lot of people can afford today, but as with all new technologies, prices tend to drop over time. You can look forward to these same treatments, and maybe even newer and more refined versions of them, becoming more widely available and affordable with each passing year. This is particularly good news for those who are dealing with acne scars, which are not typically covered by health insurance.

ADULT ACNE: THE ODDS

While teen acne affects slightly more boys than girls, the odds change as people age. Dermatologists estimate nearly 30 percent of women but only 20 percent of men over the age of 20 get breakouts.[1] These breakouts often have the same roots as teen acne, including an overproduction of androgens. Acne, particularly in later years, can also be caused by too much of the hormone estrogen. Estrogen is associated with the female reproductive system, although it is present in both genders. Adult acne particularly affects women during pregnancy and around menopause.

RISK OF BIRTH DEFECTS

Some acne treatments, especially isotretinoin, have been known to occasionally cause birth defects. Women who are considering having children should be aware of the risk and follow the advice given by their physician during their treatment period. It is important to never share medication with friends because you do not know their medical history. A prescription medicine that is helpful for one person can be dangerous for another person.

Don't let your acne stop you from enjoying life!

Getting rid of adult acne can often be tricky. Many medications are geared toward teenagers' skin, while an adult's skin tends to be drier. Therefore, should you discover acne is still following you into adulthood, it is a good idea to visit the doctor again. You can't necessarily expect what worked for you before to do so again. And if, like Dayna, you are moving away or if your current physician specializes only in teen acne, you can always ask for a recommendation for a doctor who would be more appropriate for you current situation.

SMELLING YOUR ACNE AWAY

People who prefer natural or herbal cures will be excited to learn researchers in the United Kingdom have had positive results using a solution of thyme, marigold, and myrrh in alcohol against acne-causing bacteria. These results might point the way toward a natural cure. Researchers in Australia are studying the effects of aromatherapy and essential oils in treating acne. If these areas of inquiry prove fruitful, the future of acne treatment might not only look good, it could smell great, too.

By the time you reach full adulthood, you may look back on your struggle with acne as a rite of passage. With good care and management, acne can disappear without any physical traces. And maybe having acne will have taught you a few things about how to take care of yourself and how to manage your emotions. Remember the real you is more than skin deep.

ASK YOURSELF THIS

- *Do you have an image of yourself and how you will look when you're an adult? What does it look like? How do you feel about it?*

- *Do you think you will have anything positive to say about the time you spent having acne? What would it be?*

- *Has having acne changed the way you look toward the future? In what way?*

JUST THE FACTS

Acne, also called acne vulgaris, is a skin disease characterized by overactivity of the oil glands in the skin. When pores get blocked, the oil builds up behind the clog, forming various kinds of blemishes, including whiteheads, blackheads, cysts, and nodules.

Acne can affect anyone, from babies to senior citizens. Typically, it afflicts people in their teen years and disappears by their mid-20s. Almost 85 percent of people will get acne in some form at some time in their lives.

Acne typically affects the face, neck, and shoulders, but it can appear almost anywhere on the body.

Acne is not life threatening, but it can leave permanent scars and cause various psychological and social problems, including social withdrawal, depression, anxiety, and feelings of low self-worth.

Acne is usually diagnosed by a physician, who will ask about the patient's medical history and lifestyle and perform a visual examination.

While the exact cause of acne is unknown, hormones, particularly androgens, and the *p. acnes* bacteria are thought to play key roles. Genetics appears to be a major factor in susceptibility to acne.

Stress, sweating under tight clothing, wearing greasy products on the hair and skin, and a diet high in sugar and starches can make acne worse.

Depending on the type and severity of the acne, it can be treated by over-the-counter medications, antibiotics and other prescription drugs, or a number of surgical procedures. Treatment can often involve a combination of methods.

Some particularly effective acne treatments, such as oral retinoids, can have severe side effects, and special care must be taken during the treatment period.

If not treated early and properly, acne can leave scars. These can be raised, depressed, or simply a discoloration of the skin. Some can take years to fade, but many never disappear on their own.

It is estimated approximately 10 million people in the United States develop acne scars every year. Getting rid of acne scars can require various forms of cosmetic surgery or other clinical procedures and can be quite costly.

A diet high in vitamins A, C, E, the minerals zinc and selenium, and omega-3 fatty acids has been shown to be beneficial in fighting acne.

While chocolate and fatty foods have not been shown to affect acne, stimulants such as nicotine and caffeine are thought to make acne worse.

Acne treatment is estimated to be a $3 billion industry in the United States alone.

WHERE TO TURN

If a Pimple Has Developed into a Full Face of Acne

Stay calm and resist the urge to try to scrub the pimples away or pop them. That will only make things worse and increase your risk for scarring. Likewise, feeling stressed out can also make acne worse. It is okay to try to treat mild acne with over-the-counter acne medicines, but a physician who can make recommendations for treatment should examine moderate, severe, or persistent acne. Successful treatment means less risk that acne will lead to visible and permanent scarring.

If You Have Been Diagnosed with Acne

It is important to be patient, particularly if you have severe or cystic acne. Treatment periods are measured in weeks, months, and sometimes even years. It is important you understand exactly how your treatment works, the risks involved, and what foods and activities you should avoid during the treatment period. It is also critical you learn to be aware of any new symptoms and report them to your doctor, as these may be indicative of a medication's side effects.

If You Need More Information about Your Acne

For medical advice, you can turn to your doctor, dermatologist, or other health-care professional. You can also find good information online if you restrict yourself to Web sites of known and reliable organizations. One place to start is the Mayo Clinic Web site: www.mayoclinic.com. More information can also be found at the American Academy of Dermatology Web site: www.aad.org.

If You Need Support Dealing with Your Acne

If you want to share how you feel and find out how others are coping, you can find dozens of acne forums online, as well as other people in your own community with acne. Blogs and social network connections can be helpful in this regard as well. However, never take medical advice from unknown sources online.

If You Are Feeling Depressed about Your Acne

If you are or someone you know is feeling depressed and you don't know where to turn, you can find helpful information from Mental Health America: www.nmha.org. If you need help with depression or suicide immediately, call 1-800-273-TALK. Outside the United States, you can search for a help line in your country at Befrienders Worldwide: www.befrienders.org.

If You Are Wondering about Your Future

If you are a teen struggling with acne, one of the best and happiest places to turn is to the future. Most acne does not last past a person's mid-20s. In the meantime, research and knowledge about acne and its effective treatment is advancing each day. Even if you should find your acne does persist into adulthood, the breakthrough in treatment you need could be just around the corner.

GLOSSARY

androgen
The compound responsible for the development of male sexual characteristics.

astringent
A substance that shrinks or contracts body tissue and causes secretions to dry up. Examples include alcohol, witch hazel, and calamine.

capillary
A tiny blood vessel.

carbohydrate
A substance found in certain foods that provides your body with heat and energy.

collagen
A naturally produced protein that serves as the body's "glue," holding cells or other body tissue together.

enzyme
Any of various proteins that facilitate important chemical reactions in the body.

follicle
A tiny skin organ responsible for the production of hair.

hormone
A chemical produced by an endocrine gland that travels through the bloodstream and controls body processes, including mood and behavior.

immune system
The system in the body that fights off diseases by attacking the agents that cause them.

inflammation
The body's natural response to illness, injury, pain, or stress. Blood, antibodies, and other immune substances rush in to break down damaged tissue, kill germs, and rebuild healthy tissue, causing swelling, redness, heat, pain, and/or loss of function.

nodule
A small, hard mass of tissue that usually forms after an injury.

papule
A tiny, solid bump on the skin with no visible fluid inside.

pigmentation
The natural coloring of people, animals, or plants.

sebum
A waxy, oily substance secreted by the sebaceous gland, whose function is to keep hair and skin lubricated and moist.

steroid
A hormone that performs a variety of functions in the body, from regulating the immune system to decreasing inflammation.

stimulant
A category of drugs that elevate the mood and increase alertness; includes cocaine, methamphetamine, and Ritalin.

topical
Made to be put on the skin.

ADDITIONAL RESOURCES

SELECTED BIBLIOGRAPHY

"Acne." *American Academy of Dermatology*. American Academy of Dermatology, 2013. Web. 23 Aug. 2013.

Park, Andrew. "Why Does Acne Still Exist?" *Atlantic*. Atlantic Monthly Group, 5 June 2013. Web. 23 Aug. 2013.

Watson, Stephanie. "Coping with Acne: Your Care Plan; Coping with the Emotional Impact of Acne." *WebMD*. WebMD, n.d. Web. 23 Aug. 2013.

FURTHER READINGS

Goodheart, Herbert P. *Acne for Dummies*. Indianapolis, IN: Wiley, 2006. Print.

Madaras, Lynda, and Area Madaras. *My Body, My Self for Girls*. New York: New Market, 2007. Print.

Madaras, Lynda, and Area Madaras. *The "What's Happening to My Body?" Book for Boys*. New York: Newmarket, 2007. Print.

WEB SITES

To learn more about living with acne, visit ABDO Publishing Company online at **www.abdopublishing.com**. Web sites about living with acne are featured on our Book Links page. These links are routinely monitored and updated to provide the most current information available.

SOURCE NOTES

CHAPTER 1. BREAKOUT!

1. Catherine Saint Louis. "Younger Children Seek Acne Cure." *New York Times: Well*. New York Times, 20 May 2013. Web. 23 Aug. 2013.

2. C. E. Cheng, et al. "Self-Reported Acne Severity, Treatment, and Belief Patterns across Multiple Racial and Ethnic Groups in Adolescent Students." *Pediatric Dermatology* 25.5 (Sept.–Oct. 2010): abstract. *PubMed.gov.* Web. 23 Aug. 2013.

3. "Acne." *American Academy of Dermatology*. American Academy of Dermatology, 2013. Web. 23 Aug. 2013.

CHAPTER 2. IS "ZIT" MY FAULT?

1. Elizabeth Shimer Bowers. "Coping with Acne: Your Care Plan; How Your Period Affects Acne." *WebMD*. WebMD, n.d. Web. 23 Aug. 2013.

CHAPTER 3. BEING A PATIENT ACNE PATIENT

1. Andrew Park. "Why Does Acne Still Exist?" *Atlantic.* Atlantic Monthly Group, 5 June 2013. Web. 23 Aug. 2013.

2. "6 Natural Ways to Treat Acne." *Reader's Digest.ca.* Reader's Digest Magazines Canada Limited, n.d. Web. 23 Aug. 2013.

3. Ibid.

4. Joyce Teng. Message to the author. 5 Aug. 2013. E-mail.

CHAPTER 4. SEVERE, PERSISTENT, AND CYSTIC ACNE

1. Peter Sonnereich. "American Academy of Dermatology (2011 Annual Meeting Presentation Summaries)." *Pharmacy and Therapeutics* 36.5 (May 2011). *PubMed Central.* Web. 23 Aug. 2013.

2. Thomas P. Habif. *Clinical Dermatology.* New York: Elsevier, 2010. *Google Book Search.* Web. 23 Aug. 2013.

SOURCE NOTES CONTINUED

CHAPTER 5. SCARRING

1. Christine Bowman. "Tears and Acne Scarring." *National Institute of Medical Aesthetics*. National Institute of Medical Aesthetics, 5 Feb. 2013. Web. 23 Aug. 2013.

CHAPTER 6. LIVING IN YOUR SKIN—DIET AND LIFESTYLE

None.

CHAPTER 7. PSYCHOLOGICAL, EMOTIONAL, AND SOCIAL ISSUES

1. Stephanie Watson. "Coping with Acne: Your Care Plan; Coping with the Emotional Impact of Acne." *WebMD*. WebMD, n.d. Web. 23 Aug. 2013.

2. Ibid.

CHAPTER 8. HELP, SUPPORT, AND RESOURCES

None.

CHAPTER 9. ACNE INTO ADULTHOOD

1. Charlotte Libov. "Adult Acne: Why You Get It, How to Fight It." *WebMD*. WebMD, 31 Mar. 2010. Web. 23 Aug. 2013.

INDEX

ABOUT THE AUTHOR

MK Ehrman is a freelance writer and editor. He has written numerous magazine articles and self-help books for children, teens, and adults.